THE SOUTHERN RAILWAY COLLECTION

Branch Lines Recalled

Terry Gough

• RAILWAY HERITAGE •
from
The NOSTALGIA Collection

First published 1982 as *Around The Branch Lines, No 1 Southern* by Oxford Publishing Co
New Silver Link Publishing edition first published March 1999

British Library Cataloguing in Publication Data

A catalogue record for this book is available from the British Library.

ISBN 1 85794 126 8

Silver Link Publishing Ltd
The Trundle
Ringstead Road
Great Addington
Kettering
Northants NN14 4BW

Tel/Fax: 01536 330588
email: sales@slinkp-p.demon.co.uk

Printed and bound in Great Britain

Title page: On summer Saturdays the first train from Axminster to Lyme Regis, although only two coaches, was double-headed to avoid light engine working. The engines would later be used for the up through train for London. Class 0415 Nos. 30584 and 30582 head the 8.10 am leaving Axminster on 13th August 1960.

Below: Standard Class 4MT No. 76054 on the 6.07 pm Southampton Terminus-Bournemouth Central train passes Class M7 No. 30125 on a Lymington train at Brockenhurst on 7th June 1960.

CONTENTS

INTRODUCTION

To many people the Southern Region of British Railways consisted of short-haul high-intensity services within the South East of England, and main-line trains to holiday resorts. But sandwiched within this system were rural lines, using stock and motive power from the pre-grouping companies constituting the Southern Railway. Some branches, such as Hayling Island, had hourly services, whereas others had perhaps only two or three trains per day with none on Sundays. In their latter years, some lines were allocated more modern or refurbished stock and British Railways Standard or Ivatt tank engines. A few were taken over by diesel units or were electrified, but the majority declined in importance and eventually closed. A feature common toward the end of their existence was the running of occasional special trains for ramblers and railway enthusiasts.

In this collection of photographs I have tried to capture the atmosphere of the lines in the last few years of steam working, showing the ordinary branch train and some of the more unusual workings.

This book covers those rural lines with a terminus, and services operated usually by push-pull trains – the classic branch line. I have also included minor lines worked on a branch-line basis, but connecting two main routes. I have thus drawn a distinction between, for example, the Horsham-Guildford line, which I have regarded as a branch line, and secondary routes, such as that between Tunbridge Wells West and Brighton, which are outside the scope of this book.

The comments made about the various lines refer to the period over which the photographs were taken (1956-1966) unless stated otherwise, and like all generalisations the reader will, no doubt, know of exceptions. These notes are made in order to help capture the atmosphere of branches in Southern England over the period in question. It is for this reason that I have used the 12-hour clock when quoting train times.

The book was first published in 1982, and I have taken the opportunity to make a few changes in this new edition.

Terry Gough, Sherborne, 1999

Abbreviations

BR	British Railways
GWR	Great Western Railway
IWCR	Isle of Wight Central Railway
LBSCR	London, Brighton & South Coast Railway
LCDR	London, Chatham & Dover Railway
LMSR	London Midland & Scottish Railway

LSWR	London & South Western Railway
SDJR	Somerset & Dorset Joint Railway
SECR	South Eastern & Chatham Railway
SER	South Eastern Railway
SR	Southern Railway
WD	War Department

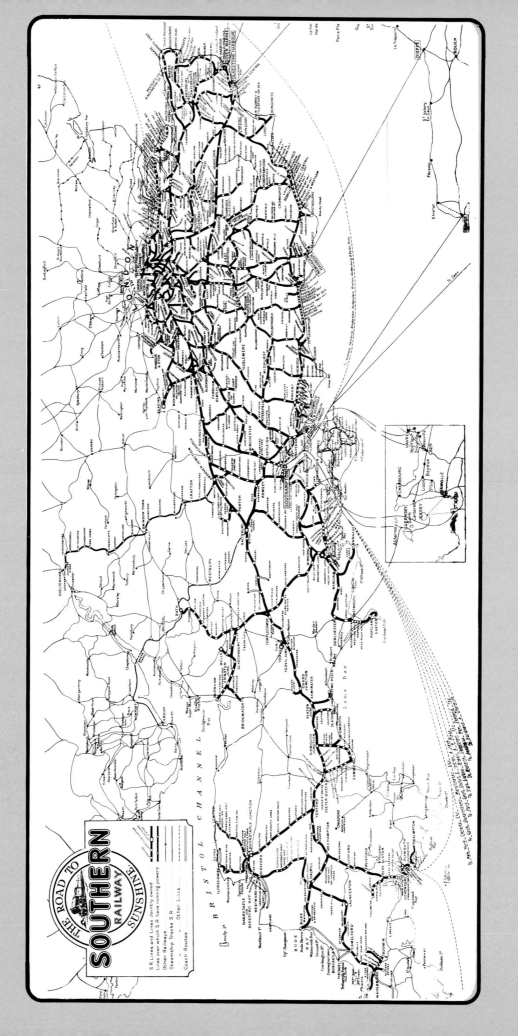

THE ALLHALLOWS-ON-SEA BRANCH

The original line to Port Victoria was built in the hope of generating substantial traffic from the port itself. An SECR map issued about 1913 showed Port Victoria as the departure point for services to Holland, Germany and Northern Europe in general. In 1932 the Southern Railway opened a spur to the new resort of Allhallows-on-Sea. Neither the shipping nor the holiday traffic materialised. The Port Victoria line was cut back to Grain in 1951, where an oil refinery had been built and 10 years later Allhallows itself was closed.

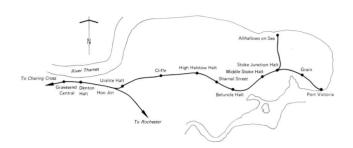

Plate 1: All trains normally started from Gravesend Central and most were push-pull operated. This is typified by SECR Class H No. 31322 and an ex-LBSCR two-coach set seen here on 13th September 1959.

Plate 3: Sharnal Street was one of the main intermediate stations. On Saturdays the 10.37 am from Gravesend ran with the engine sandwiched between two push-pull sets. The rear set was dropped at Sharnal Street and propelled by another engine to Grain as empty carriage stock. It then formed the 11.50 am workmen's train back to Gravesend. Class H No. 31177 is seen with sets Nos. 714 and 735 on 24th September 1960.

Plate 2 (top left): The branch left the North Kent line at Hoo Junction. Class H No. 31518 is on the 2.24 pm from Allhallows, passing Hoo Junction Railway Staff Halt on 14th October 1961. The halt served the adjacent marshalling yards. To enable electric locomotives to use the yard, overhead rather than third rail pick-up was installed, thus making it operationally much safer.

Plate 4 (right): Class Q1 No. 33037 at Beluncle Halt on an oil train from Grain to Hoo Junction on 24th September 1960. It was the refinery which saved the line from complete closure, although passenger traffic ceased at the end of 1961.

Plate 5 (below): The same Q1 later in the day, with one Maunsell coach and an SR utility van, forming the 1.44 pm Gravesend–Allhallows at Sharnal Street.

Plate 8 (right):   Allhallows, with its characteristic water tower and caravans in the background. Class H No. 31519 leaves for Gravesend on 12th September 1959 with ex-SECR railmotor set No. 481 (see also *Plate 164*).

Plate 6 (below):   Another Q1, No. 33036 on an Allhallows train at Stoke Junction Halt, where the Grain line diverged. The halt was opened the same year as the Allhallows spur and the photograph shows the original buildings.

Plate 7 (below):   All the original halts on the line were rebuilt by the SR, using pre-cast concrete, to a particularly uninspiring design. Class H No. 31530 arrives at Middle Stoke Halt on 2nd December 1961.

Plate 9: The 2nd December 1961 was the penultimate day of passenger services. Class H No. 31324 approaches Stoke Junction Halt from Allhallows. The Grain line is in the foreground. The stock consists of Maunsell coaches, converted by BR to push-pull operation.

THE BEXHILL WEST BRANCH

Bexhill West was the terminus of a short SECR branch from Crowhurst. It was built to main line proportions and was an attempt to compete with the LBSCR line also serving the resort of Bexhill. Patronage was poor throughout most of the line's existence, despite a frequent service connecting with London–Hastings trains.

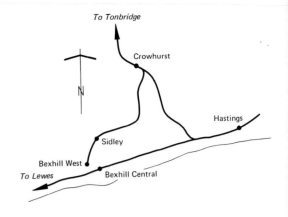

Plate 10: The grandeur of Bexhill West emphasised by the insignificance of the branch train. Class H No. 31519 on the 4.26 pm to Crowhurst on 3rd June 1958.

Plate 11 (right upper): Class H No. 31162 at Sidley, the only intermediate station, propelling push-pull set No. 661 toward ▶ Bexhill West on the same day.

Plate 12 (right lower): The line was dieselised at the same time as the main line, and diesel electric unit No. 1119 is seen in ▶ the background at Bexhill West. Class E1 No. 31019 is arriving on the evening of 19th October 1958 with an excursion from west London. The stock is a Maunsell restriction 'O' Hastings line set.

THE BORDON BRANCH AND
THE LONGMOOR MILITARY RAILWAY

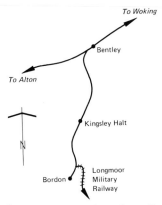

A short branch left the Woking–Alton line at Bentley to serve Bordon, which was at the northern end of the Longmoor Military Railway. The line was worked for many years by an LSWR Class M7 0-4-4 tank engine from Guildford and a push-pull set.

Plate 13: Set No. 384 at Bordon on 29th March 1956. The station buildings are rather uninspiring, but the rolling stock is interesting in that it consists of main line coaches built for the through services from Waterloo to Lymington and Swanage. There were five such sets, Nos. 381–385, each consisting of a brake third and a brake composite. They were built by the Southern Railway in 1925 to an LSWR design and were known as Ironclads because the bodies were steel sheeted. In 1949 all the sets had their outer corridor connections removed and were converted to push-pull operation.

Plate 14 (right upper): Long after withdrawal of passenger services, the branch saw occasional specials. Class M7 No. 30028 and set No. 1 approach Bentley from Bordon on a Hampshire branches tour special on 15th October 1960.

Plate 15 (right lower): A through train from the Longmoor Railway joining the LSWR at Bordon in April 1966. The Longmoor Military Railway, which was an extensive system used by the armed services mainly for training purposes, also had connections with British Railways at Liss on the Waterloo–Portsmouth main line.

Plate 16: The same train leaving the Bordon branch. The WD Class 2-10-0, named *Gordon*, with its modern rolling stock, makes an interesting contrast to the train in *Plate 14*.

Plate 17: A special railway enthusiasts' train on the Longmoor Military Railway in 1966, hauled by Austerity 0-6-0 No. 196, in the guise of BR Class J94 No 68011.

◀ *Plate 18:* Longmoor Down station, with No. 196 shunting a train of Bulleid coaches.

◀ *Plate 19:* The remarkable sight of Class 9F No. 92203 on the Longmoor Military Railway with a special train a few months before closure of the railway.

Plate 20: A special train in April 1996 made several trips round the Longmoor Military Railway; the odd make-up of the train can be seen here.

Plate 21: Two Class O1s, Nos. 31065 and 31258, shunting at Shepherdswell in April 1960.

THE EAST KENT RAILWAY

Shepherdswell was the beginning of the East Kent Railway which threaded its way through the Kentish coal fields. There was a passenger service from Shepherdswell to Eastry and Wingham, consisting of two mixed trains per day. The EKR was closed to passenger services in 1948, but the presence of the collieries ensured that freight operation continued, under BR ownership, for many years.

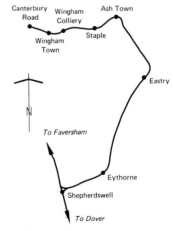

Plate 22 (right upper): The interchange yard at Shepherdswell was fitted for overhead electric pick-up during the Kent ▶ electrification scheme. On 21st April 1960 Class O1 No. 31065 is seen in the foreground. In the background is a BR Type 2 (later Class 24) diesel No. D5002. This was one of fifteen allocated to the Southern Region.

Plate 23 (right lower): A portrait of old world charm. Class O1 No. 31065 poses on 21st April 1960. ▶

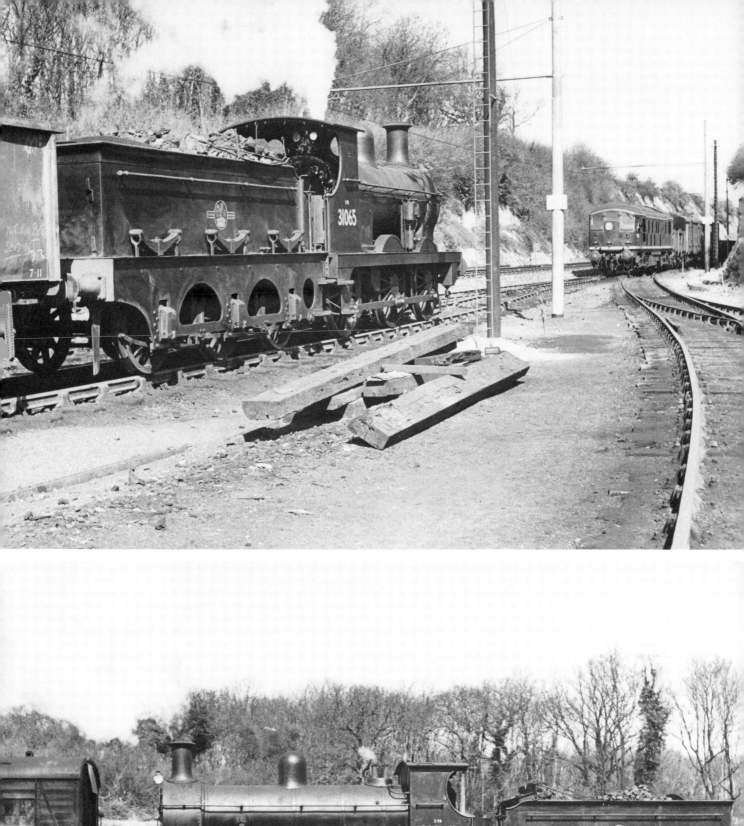

Plate 24: The EKR was worked by O1s for many years and Nos. 31065 and 31258 are seen near the site of the EKR passenger station on 21st April 1960. There were 59 of these engines, rebuilt from the Stirling class O. Most were withdrawn in 1949 and 1950, although eight survived into the 1960s. Three were sold to the EKR, but these were also withdrawn shortly after nationalisation.

THE EXMOUTH BRANCH

A direct route, following the River Exe, ran from Exeter to Exmouth, leaving the main line at Exmouth Junction where a large motive power depot was situated. The line acted both as a commuter service for people working in Exeter, and, in the summer months, as a holiday route to the coast. The scenery was uninteresting and most trains were latterly formed of Standard 2-6-2 tanks and BR non-corridor stock. The line is still in operation and is worked by Western Region diesel multiple units, usually right through from Barnstaple. Exmouth could also be reached from Sidmouth Junction and this line left the Sidmouth branch at Tipton St. John's. The scenery was much more attractive than the direct route to Exmouth.

Plate 25: Standard Class 3MT No. 82024 on the 2.50 pm Exmouth–Sidmouth Junction at Budleigh Salterton on 9th August 1960. This was the other route into Exmouth by rail, but is now closed.

Plate 26: Standard Class 3MT No. 82018 on the 8.50 am Tipton St. John's–Exmouth near Littleham on 12th August 1960.

Plate 27 (left): An unidentified Class 3MT on the 9.52 am Exmouth–Sidmouth Junction crosses a small overbridge near Budleigh Salterton on 12th August 1960. The train is conveying two through coaches for Waterloo.

Plate 28 (right upper): A reminder of earlier days, with Class M7 No. 30676 arriving at Exmouth on the 11.15 am from Exeter Central on 12th August 1960. Class 2MT No. 41308 is in the background. Exmouth had a fine array of LSWR wooden-arm lower quadrant signals, some of which are seen here.

Plate 29 (right lower): The same M7 with Maunsell set No. 27, forming the 11.50 am to Tipton St. John's at Exmouth on 12th August 1960. Part of the site of Exmouth station has been given over to road development and the present station, which is much smaller, is about 80 yards nearer Exeter.

Plate 30 (above): A typical Exmouth–Exeter train, with Class 3MT No. 82025 and a five-coach BR set leaving Exmouth on 12th August 1960. Diesel operation began a year after this photograph was taken.

Plate 31: The 1.25 pm from Exeter Central ran only as far as Topsham. Class 3MT No. 82010 running round set No. 178 prior to the return working on 12th August 1960. In the background an ancient LSWR grounded coach body can just be seen.

Plate 32: An Exeter bound train with Class 3MT No. 82025 approaching Topsham. A short branch ran from this end of the station to the quay. This was closed in 1957, but the track bed can still be seen on the right beyond the buffer stop.

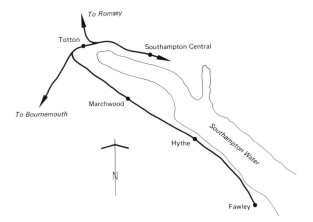

THE FAWLEY BRANCH

The branch was built by the Southern Railway and was opened on 20th July 1925 as a light railway. It left the Southampton–Bournemouth line just beyond Totton and ran parallel with Southampton Water for almost 10 miles. The service was mainly for the benefit of workers at the oil refinery and was very infrequent. On weekdays there was only one down train, but three up trains, and on Sundays there was no service at all. There was, and indeed still is, a substantial oil traffic. Passenger traffic was withdrawn in February 1966.

Plate 33 (above): Class M7 No. 30479 and a three-coach ex-LSWR non-corridor set at Fawley on 25th July 1956. Note the sliding doors on the luggage compartment and the guard's ducket on the nearest coach.

Plate 34: Ten years later, on 20th March 1966, a railway enthusiasts' special paid a visit to the branch. It is seen here crossing an ungated road near Marchwood. The motive power consists of two USA tanks, Nos. 30073 and 30064. There were 14 of this class, provided by the United States in 1946 for use primarily in Southampton Docks, where they worked for most of their existence.

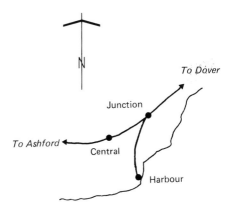

FOLKESTONE HARBOUR BRANCH

The Folkestone Harbour branch has always held an attraction for photographers, partly because of the incongruous appearance of tank engines on boat trains destined for London, and also because of the attractive setting of the harbour. The SECR Class R1 tanks, which worked the boat trains up to Folkestone Junction for many years, were replaced by GWR Class 5700 Pannier tanks in 1958.

Plate 35: Class R1 No. 31339 shunting at Folkestone Junction on 10th April 1957. This engine formerly worked the Canterbury and Whitstable line. Tyler Hill tunnel on this line had a very narrow bore, hence the lowered cab roof and chimney.

Plate 37 (right upper): Class 5700 No. 4616 banking the same train. The two rear vehicles are SR utility vans. ▶

Plate 38 (right lower): Derelict Class R1s Nos. 31128, 31047, 31010 and 31107 at Folkestone Junction shed on 26th March ▶ 1959. No. 31010 is another of the R1s having a low Stirling-type cab. To the left of the engines is an SECR water crane.

Plate 36: The 1.20pm Folkestone Harbour—Victoria double headed by Class 5700 Nos. 4630 and 4601 on 26th March 1959.

Plate 40 (right upper): Class M7 No. 30111, also at Fareham, on a special push-pull tour of Hampshire branches, with set No. 6 on 7th March 1959. The problem with most branch lines was that there were very few passengers. The drawback to photographing railway enthusiasts' specials was that there were far too many passengers. ▶

Plate 41 (right lower): Another drawback to specials was that they often ran to interesting places after dark. The same train returning from Gosport at Fort Brockhurst in failing light. Even the gas lamp has been lit, although its meagre light is of little help. Fort Brockhurst was also the junction for the branch to Lee-on-Solent. ▶

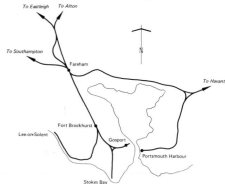

THE GOSPORT BRANCH

This line was one of the least photographically attractive of the Hampshire branches. It was built to main line standards, being envisaged that it would form (to Stokes Bay) a main line from London to the Isle of Wight via the Meon Valley. In the 1960s it was frequented by steam-worked specials, bringing by far the greatest number of passengers seen in many years.

Plate 39: On 30th April 1961 Classes O2 No. 30200 and E1 No. 32694 are seen leaving Fareham for Gosport on a special. The line to the right goes to Portsmouth Harbour. This is now a diesel service and runs to Salisbury.

HALWILL–TORRINGTON

Rail services at Halwill were out of all proportion to the population of the village they served. The reason was that it was the junction for the main LSWR routes from London to Bude and Padstow, both served by the 'Atlantic Coast Express'. It was also the junction for a branch line to Torrington, built by the Southern Railway to light railway standards. The service to Torrington has always been sparse, with only two trains on weekdays and none on Sundays. A third train ran from Torrington, only as far as Petrockstow, almost halfway to Halwill. There were large clay deposits in the Petrockstow area and indeed the line from Torrington to Marland Quarry is still open for freight traffic. In Southern Railway days clay was taken by rail to Fremington Quay which is situated between Torrington and Barnstaple. From here it was exported.

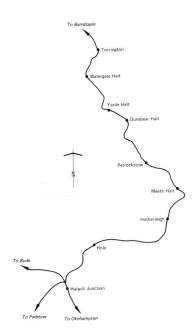

Plate 42:   The Torrington train ran from a separate platform at Halwill. Class 2MT No. 41298 is seen on the 6.40 pm to Torrington on 5th July 1961. Class N No. 31833 shunts refrigerated container vans into the local abattoir, which, judging by the noise, dealt mainly with pigs.

Plate 43 (right upper):   The 3.55 pm from Torrington approaches Halwill with Class 2MT No. 41298 on the same day There were four halts and three stations between these two points, one oddly named Hole and another Yarde.

Plate 44 (right lower):   Class 2MT No. 41298 running round the single Bulleid BCK coach (No. 6727) which was adequat for the branch. A few years previously the train would have been composed of an ex-LSWR Class M7 and one of the famou and attractive 'gate' coaches, similar to those shown in *Plate 176*.

Plate 45: A pick-up freight, including clay wagons, from Torrington at Halwill, hauled by Class 2MT No. 41295. Even freight trains used the branch bay.

THE HAWKHURST BRANCH

The branch, which was 11½ miles long, diverged at Paddock Wood on the Tonbridge–Ashford main line. It was characteristic of so many branches, having its station literally miles from the nearest village and having an irregular and infrequent service most of its history. The times remained virtually unchanged from before the War up to closure in 1961. On weekdays there were only four trains each way during sociable hours and on Sundays there was no service. It was, as a result, a difficult branch to cover photographically. The service was push-pull operated and usually worked by a Class H tank engine.

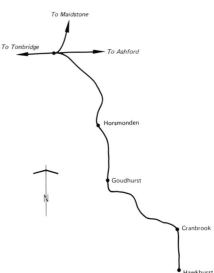

Plate 46 (right upper): Class H No. 31500 at Paddock Wood on 10th September 1960. Although this class was of SECR origin, they were found all over South East England. There were 66 members of the class built between 1904 and 1915. Even in 1955, 56 remained, of which 31 were push-pull fitted. Some were converted to push-pull working as late as 1960.

Plate 47 (right lower): Occasionally an SECR Class C was used, particularly on extra trains during the hop picking season. Such trains were guaranteed to provide ancient motive power and stock. Class C No. 31244 is seen leaving Paddock Wood on 18th September 1960.

Plate 48: The same train on a return working from Hawkhurst. Note the line passing under Paddock Wood Signal Box.

Plate 49: Class C No. 31244 again, this time a year previously on 20th August 1959. This is the daily freight train from Hawkhurst, passing the Paddock Wood fixed distant which is of SECR origin. The freight service had been diesel operated for a short while, but considerable problems (perhaps man-made?) were encountered and the service reverted to steam operation.

Plate 50: Horsmonden Station with Class C No. 31588 in charge of the 2.15 pm Paddock Wood–Hawkhurst on 10th June 1961, the last day of passenger services.

Plate 51: Set 656 on the rear of a five-coach train at Horsmonden. On this, the last day, push-pull operation was suspended and all trains were strengthened using non push-pull stock.

Plate 52: Cranbrook was the most attractive of all the stations and the view from the nearby overbridge was particularly good. On 10th June 1961 Class C No. 31588 makes an impressive start with a five-coach train heading for Hawkhurst.

Plate 53: Under normal circumstances a two-coach set was more than ample. Class H No. 31263 is seen at Cranbrook on the 4.25 pm from Paddock Wood on 10th September 1960.

Plate 54: A beautiful clear afternoon on 10th September 1960 found Class H No. 31263 heading for Hawkhurst in typical Kentish surroundings.

Plate 55: The day following the cessation of regular services saw a special at Hawkhurst in atrocious weather, double headed by Classes C No. 31592 and O1 No. 31065. This O1 was the last South Eastern Railway Stirling engine and it was withdrawn two weeks after working this train. It was later purchased for preservation. The Class C engine was also purchased privately and is now on the Bluebell Railway.

THE HAYLING ISLAND BRANCH

A short branch to Hayling Island left the Waterloo–Portsmouth main line at Havant. It served the popular holiday resort of the same name and on summer Saturdays there were 17 trains in each direction, many of them packed to capacity. There was also a bus service between the two locations. The road from Havant to Hayling Island crossed the railway at Langston and one could often see buses waiting at the level crossing or caught in traffic jams as the train made the journey in a mere 13 minutes. Despite this, the bus has won the day and as a final insult even started from the site of the branch bay at Havant for some years after closure.

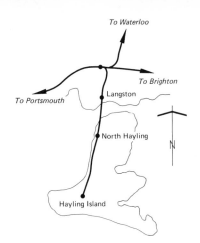

Plate 56:   Class A1X Nos. 32670 and 32650 double heading the empty carriage stock from Fratton–Havant, prior to working separately on the branch on 8th September 1963. Note that the leading Maunsell coach is from a disbanded push-pull set, the remaining two coaches being BR standard non-corridor stock.

Plate 57 (right upper):   Class A1X No. 32650 on the 2.05 pm from Havant near Langston Station on 2nd November 1963. The line used A1Xs exclusively, which were shedded at Fratton.

Plate 58 (right lower):   The same engine on the 10.52 am from Hayling Island approaching Langston Bridge on 2nd November 1963. The rolling stock seems to dwarf the engine, but for their size they were powerful machines. There were originally 21 of the class, being rebuilt from the Stroudley Class A1. Even today several still exist in working order.

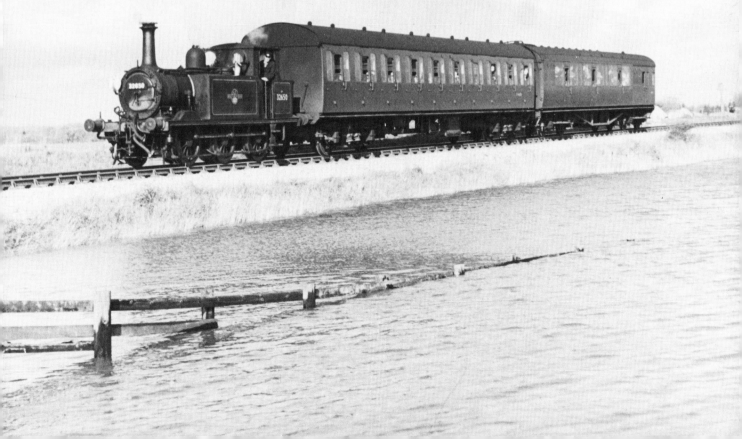

◄ *Plate 59 (left upper):*   Class A1X No. 32678 with the 3.35 pm from Havant on Langston Bridge on 21st August 1960. It was the poor structural state of this bridge which contributed towards the closure of the line at the end of 1963.

◄ *Plate 60 (left lower):*   Twilight on the Hayling Island branch. Class A1X No. 32650 crosses Langston Bridge on 3rd November 1963, the day before closure.

Plate 61 (above):   The other intermediate station on the branch was North Hayling, which was nothing more than a small wooden halt, so common all along the South Coast. Class A1X No. 32650 pulls away on the 10.19 am from Havant on 10th October 1963.

Plate 62 (overleaf):   Hayling Island on the summer evening of 30th August 1959. Class A1X No. 32640 is arriving on the 6.05 pm from Havant and No. 32661 is ready to leave on the 6.40 pm to Havant. Despite the intensive service, at this time of day all trains were packed to capacity with homeward bound holidaymakers and day trippers.

Plate 63: Another summer scene at Hayling Island, with Class A1X No. 32670, on 21st August the following year. Note that one of the LBSCR starters shown in *Plate 62* has been replaced by an SR rail-built signal.

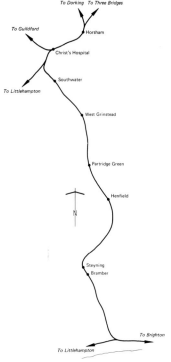

HORSHAM—BRIGHTON

The direct electric service was not the only way to reach Brighton from London. More leisurely routes were to be found both to the east and west of the main line. Suburban trains could be used as far as Horsham, followed by the steam-operated service on to Brighton.

Plate 64 (right upper): Class E4 No. 32503 and Maunsell set No. 952 leaving Christ's Hospital on the 5.19 pm Horsham—Brighton on 24th March 1961. This station, built mainly to serve the public school of the same name, is the first station out of Horsham and was also served by electric trains to Littlehampton and steam trains to Guildford. Like so many LBSCR stations it was built on a grand scale, far bigger than could ever be justified for the amount of traffic forthcoming. ▶

Plate 65 (right lower): On 27th July 1963, Class 2MT No. 41325 is seen on the 11.21 am Horsham—Brighton approaching Itchingfield Junction. It was here that the Littlehampton and Brighton lines diverged. The gantry shows a distant signal for the branch, a fairly unusual arrangement on the SR (see also *Plate 122*). The train is composed of Bulleid set No. 92. ▶

◄ *Plate 66 (left upper):* Even 'West Country' Class Pacifics were occasionally seen on the branch. No. 34070 *Manston* leaves Southwater with a 'Ramblers' Excursion' from Victoria on 24th July 1960.

◄ *Plate 67 (left lower):* Another special working, this time on 22nd March 1964 and for railway enthusiasts. Class N No. 31411 is seen leaving West Grinstead. There were 80 locomotives of this class, which was introduced by Maunsell in 1927. They could be found all over the Southern system, from Kent to Cornwall, but were rare visitors to this line.

Plate 68 (above): Class M7 No. 30049 with an all-third coach and push-pull set near Partridge Green on 24th March 1960.

Plate 69 (left upper): The same train, three years later on 27th July 1963, with modern motive power and stock. Class 2MT No. 41230 and three-coach Bulleid set No. 92 at Partridge Green. Modern stock was no doubt much more comfortable than some of the pre-grouping stock used on this line, but was less photogenic.

Plate 70 (left lower): Class H No. 31322 with Maunsell set No. 601 and a loose all-third coach on the 4.19 pm from Horsham at Bramber on 24th July 1960. The ironwork of the footbridge is reflected in the windows of the first-class compartments.

Plate 71 (above): Class M7 No. 30052 at Steyning on 24th July 1960. This station was only half a mile from Bramber. The pause for water, obtained from an LBSCR column, was after allowing passengers to join the train. When the train was being pushed, as in this instance, it precluded the photographer from continuing his journey by train.

Plate 72 (above): There was always a surprising amount of steam activity at Brighton, despite being served predominantly by electric trains. Class E4 No. 32512 is about to depart on the 12.30 pm to Horsham on 22nd April 1961.

Plate 73 (left): The incoming working (11.19 am ex-Horsham) was made by another Class E4, No. 32468. Class E4s were uncommon on this service and to have two simultaneously was most unusual.

Plate 74 (right upper): A fine start for Class E4 No. 32475 which has just left Christ's Hospital on the 3.09 pm to Guildford on 24th March 1961.

Plate 75 (right lower): The same engine on an evening train on 24th March 1961 from Guildford, near Christ's Hospital. Class E4s were not push-pull fitted, although push-pull stock was often used on the branch until the last few years of operation.

HORSHAM–GUILDFORD

The line was opened in 1865 and gave LBSCR trains access to the LSWR at Guildford. Despite hope that the line would be used as a route from the Midlands to Brighton, very little through traffic was ever seen. By nationalisation, the line was nothing more than a country branch, with a poorly patronised passenger service and a daily pick-up freight. This was surprising, bearing in mind that the line connected two towns of considerable importance, whose road connection was poor and even now, after the loss of the railway, is little better.

Plate 76: Class M7 No. 30132 on a pick-up freight from Guildford at Baynards on 24th March 1961. There were private sidings here, where there was a Fullers' Earth works, which created considerable traffic for the railway.

Plate 77 (right upper): Class 2MT No. 41303 on the 12.09 pm from Horsham at Baynards. Although there was a hamlet of this name, the station was built mainly to serve the nearby country estate.

Plate 78 (right lower): Class E4 No. 32475 leaving Baynards on the 10.34 am from Guildford on 24th March 1961. Baynards was a most attractive station, but by this time was unfortunately serving very little purpose.

Plate 79 (left): On Saturdays only, the 1.09 pm from Guildford ran only as far as Cranleigh, returning to Guildford after a stop of 10 minutes. Motive power was provided by Guildford shed and seemed to be whatever was available. Class 700 No. 30697 is seen running round set No. 663 at Cranleigh on 2nd April 1960. Note the substantial wooden-posted signal with a calling-on arm.

Plate 80 (left): Trains passing at Bramley and Wonersh on 2nd April 1960. Class 700 No. 30697 is returning to Guildford and set No. 606 is being propelled by a Class H tank.

Plate 81 (upper): Running round at Guildford. Class 2MT No. 41287 with set No. 90 after working the 3.09 pm from Horsham on 22nd August 1964. The stock is situated by the side of the main line to Portsmouth. In the foreground is the line from Reading and the line curving away in the background is the so-called 'New Line' to Waterloo via Effingham Junction.

Plate 82 (below): The 9.30 am from Horsham emerging from Guildford Tunnel with Class M7 No. 30328 hauling set No. 606 and an all-third loose coach. The engine shed, on the right, was sandwiched between the station and the tunnel. For many years the shed was out of bounds to visitors, as most of the roof was missing. It was, however, possible to see what was on shed by climbing up the path on the hill behind the shed. By the time this photograph was taken, on 27th August 1960, it had been replaced.

Plate 83: A year or so before closure, more modern stock was introduced. Class 2MT No. 41301 and set No. 771 are approaching Guildford on the 4.53 pm from Horsham on 15th May 1964. The signal box behind the train is a standard LSWR main line design.

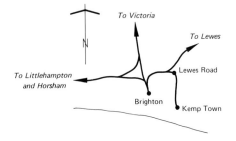

THE KEMP TOWN BRANCH

Plate 84: Kemp Town, surrounded by the electrified lines along the South Coast, was closed to passenger traffic before the Second World War, but occasionally saw special workings. Class Q No. 30530 approaches Kemp Town on the final stage of a tour of Sussex lines on the evening of 18th October 1964. The Q Class were built to the design of Maunsell in 1938 as freight locomotives, but for some reason were favourites for railway enthusiasts' specials.

THE KENT AND EAST SUSSEX RAILWAY

The KESR was probably the most famous of all the Colonel Stephens' railways. It was operated by the Southern Railway and later by BR in two sections. The northern part of the line from Headcorn Junction to Rolvenden was worked by Class O1 0-6-0 tender engines and the southern part by ex-LBSCR Class A1X tank engines. The service was third class only and apart from once per day, there was no connecting service between the two sections of the line. When the author travelled on the line on the last day, he was nevertheless able to buy a Kent and East Sussex Railway first-class ticket. Long after withdrawal of regular passenger services, there were occasional summer excursions on the southern end of the line, which left the London–Hastings main line at Robertsbridge. Part of this section is still in operation as a preserved railway.

Plate 85: Class A1X No. 32670 with a train at Tenterden on 18th October 1959. This was the only town of any size on the line and was the point at which most trains for Robertsbridge started.

Plate 86:   A special train, to mark the end of steam in Kent, visited Rolvenden, hauled by Class A1X No. 32662 on 11th June 1961. Rolvenden was the headquarters of the KESR, which had a small works and engine shed here. Headcorn-bound trains usually started from Rolvenden, thus there was an overlap with the Robertsbridge service on the short section between here and Tenterden.

Plate 87:   Stock from the same train taken over by Classes H No. 31308 and D1 No. 31749 at Robertsbridge. The diesel electric unit is No. 1019.

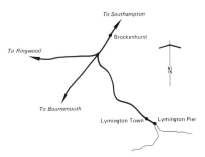

THE LYMINGTON BRANCH

The branch, which was opened in 1858, has always been of considerable importance as a gateway to the Isle of Wight. For many years it was worked by Class M7 tank engines and Ironclad push-pull sets (see *Plate 13*). Trains ran from Brockenhurst and left the Bournemouth main line, and simultaneously the Ringwood line, at Lymington Junction. There were also through services from Waterloo to Lymington on summer Saturdays. Steam lasted until 1967, but instead of the usual fate of branch lines, the service was continued with diesel electric units. This only lasted for a few months until completion of the laying of the third rail. From then onward, the branch has enjoyed a frequent service operated by electric units.

Plate 88: Class M7 No. 30028 and set No. 384 leaving Brockenhurst on the 10.58 am to Lymington Pier on 30th August 1961. The footbridge gives an excellent view of the railway and leads to a footpath which runs alongside the extensive goods yard, towards Lymington Junction.

Plate 89: The line from Brockenhurst climbs all the way to the junction. Class M7 No. 30125 pushes its train out of Brockenhurst on the 1 in 76 past the yard on 7th June 1960.

Plate 90: Lymington Junction with set No. 384 on the 4.01 pm from Lymington Pier on 10th September 1959. Beyond the junction the line crosses that part of the New Forest known as Setley Plain, which is virtually devoid of trees. There is little of photographic interest until the line reaches Lymington Town.

Plate 91: For many years Lymington Town was the only intermediate station, although in 1956 a halt was opened to serve a local factory estate just outside Lymington. On 7th June 1960 Class M7 No. 30125 is seen leaving Lymington Town on the 4.18 pm to Brockenhurst.

Plate 92: Class Q1 No 33006 approaches Lymington Town on a London-bound special train on the evening of 20th March 1966.

Plate 94 (right upper):   At Axminster on 13th August 1960, the through coaches from Lyme Regis to Waterloo are being attached to the rear of the main line train from Exeter, using Class 0415 No. 30584.

Plate 95 (right lower):   Class 0415 Nos. 30584 and 30582 with five Bulleid coaches on the 3.05 pm Lyme Regis–Waterloo, struggling round the curve near the terminus on the wet afternoon of 13th August 1960.

THE LYME REGIS BRANCH

This was probably the most well known and most photographed line in the South of England, due to the presence of the ex-LSWR Class 0415 4-4-2 tank engines and rather attractive scenery. Another feature was that the branch bay at Axminster was on the up side of the main line. The branch crossed the main line by an overbridge just beyond the station. The line abounded in tight curves and steep gradients, hence the retention of the radial tanks. However, some realignment was carried out in the 1960s, which resulted in their demise and replacement by more modern motive power.

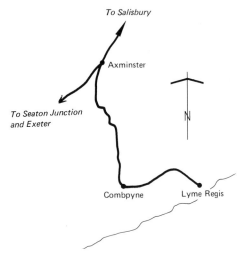

Plate 93 (below):   Portrait of Class 0415 No. 30584 in the bay at Axminster on 31st July 1957. There were originally 71 of this class, designed by Adams for the LSWR suburban services. By 1928 they had all been withdrawn, except for one which worked on the East Kent Railway, and two which were retained at Exmouth Junction motive power depot for the Lyme Regis line.

Plate 98 (above): After being displaced by ex-LMSR tank engines, the through trains no longer needed to be double headed. Class 2MT No. 41292 stands with the 10.10 am to Waterloo at Lyme Regis on 8th July 1961.

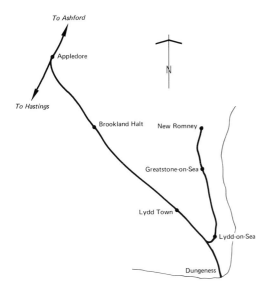

THE NEW ROMNEY BRANCH

  The New Romney Branch left the Ashford—Hastings line at Appledore, a typical SECR country station with staggered platforms. Originally the line, which crossed Romney Marsh, divided at Lydd, one part continuing to Dungeness and the other turning north-east to New Romney. Dungeness never became the resort once anticipated and in 1937 the Southern Railway closed the junction at Lydd and re-sited the connection to New Romney three-quarters of a mile from Dungeness. At the same time this short length into Dungeness was closed and new stations were opened at Greatstone-on-Sea and Lydd-on-Sea. The original Lydd was renamed Lydd Town.

◄ *Plate 96 (left upper):*   More typical of the branch trains was the 11.39 am to Lyme Regis, seen near Combpyne and headed by Class 0415 No. 30582 on 13th August 1960.

◄ *Plate 97 (left lower):*   So quiet was Combpyne that one could be led to believe that the sole purpose of the station was to provide the camping coach clientele. Class 0415 No. 30582 is seen leaving Combpyne three years earlier on the 3.31 pm from Axminster. The camping coach is in the background.

Plate 99: Most of the branch workings were through trains from Ashford, consisting of two-coach ex-LBSCR push-pull sets and a Class H 0-4-4 tank engine. No. 31279 is seen at Appledore on 3rd June 1958.

Plate 100 (right upper): Class H No. 31521 leaving Brookland Halt, the first and one of the original stations on the branch, early on the morning of 5th September 1956.

Plate 101 (right lower): Class H No. 31310 on the 12.47 pm Ashford—New Romney at Ham Street and Orlestone, which is before the junction for the branch itself, on 3rd June 1958.

Plate 103 (right upper): Class H No. 31520 on the 2.10 pm Tonbridge—Maidstone West at Paddock Wood on 20th August ▶ 1959. Paddock Wood was one of the most interesting stations in Kent with trains for both branches, local services between Tonbridge and Dover, expresses and boat trains from London to Folkestone and Dover, and an extensive yard. A down express is signalled on the through line.

Plate 104 (right lower): Sitting in the sun by the steps of Paddock Wood signal box on 10th September 1960 gave an ▶ excellent view of the 11.48 am Maidstone—Tonbridge train with set No. 663 and on the front Class H No. 31553. On the left the Hawkhurst train waits to depart.

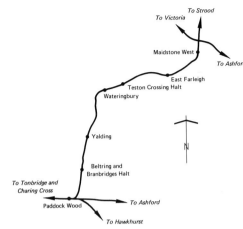

PADDOCK WOOD—MAIDSTONE

Paddock Wood was the junction for the line to Maidstone West as well as for Hawkhurst. Normally, trains were push-pull operated and started either at Paddock Wood itself or Tonbridge. Many branch lines were closed before the commuting population was forced further and further from London by rising house prices. However, the Paddock Wood—Maidstone line survived and is now part of the outer suburban electric service to London.

Plate 102: All ex-LCDR Class R1 tanks were withdrawn by the early 1950s except No. 31704, seen here at Paddock Wood with set No. 723 on a Maidstone West train on 3rd April 1956. The engine was withdrawn a few days later. The down train from Charing Cross is seen on the left.

Plate 105: A hop pickers' special from London Bridge to stations on the Maidstone line leaving Paddock Wood behind Class C No. 31693 on 18th September 1960. The hop picking season lasted only a couple of weeks but it was well worth a visit to Kent during this period.

Plate 106: On the same day, scheduled trains were strengthened to accommodate hop pickers. Class H No. 31518 on the 10.35 am from Tonbridge–Maidstone with sets Nos. 610 (Maunsell) and 653 (LSWR), both converted to push-pull working in later years. In the up platform is the branch train from Maidstone.

Plate 107 (above): The rare sight of a double headed train on the branch. Classes L1 No. 31786 and D1 No. 31749 approach Paddock Wood on 10th June 1961, the day before electrification. The Class D1s were Maunsell rebuilds of original express engines designed by Wainwright, whereas the L1s were new engines based on the Wainwright Class L.

Plate 108 (below): Wateringbury was a most attractive station, enhanced by the presence of Class H No. 31184 on an ex-LBSCR push-pull set en route to Maidstone on 4th September 1956.

Plate 109: Class D1 No. 31487 on a hop pickers friends' train near Wateringbury on 13th September 1959. The story is that hop pickers came to pick next year's supply of beer, whereas their friends came to drink last year's crop. Neither of the Maunsell coaches had brake vans and so an SR four-wheeled brake/luggage van was added to the train. The concrete blocks littering the embankment are for covering cables associated with the imminent electrification.

Plate 110: Class C No. 31287 is seen heading a Tonbridge-bound freight through East Farleigh on 20th September 1959. This station is in pleasant wooded surroundings.

PULBOROUGH–MIDHURST

Midhurst was the main town on the line connecting Pulborough and Petersfield. The first section was LBSCR and the remainder was LSWR, with two separate stations at Midhurst itself. Even in British Railways days the two services were run almost independently, although all trains started from the former LBSCR station at Midhurst. After the cessation of passenger services there were still occasional special trains between Pulborough and Midhurst.

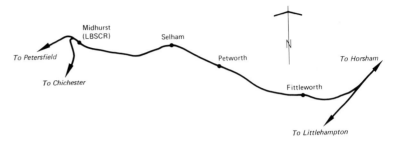

Plate 111: A special train near Fittleworth on 18th October 1964, returning from a visit to Midhurst. The engine is Class Q No. 30530 and the stock is special traffic set No. 770. Tour trains were usually self sufficient in that buffet facilities were provided, in this case using one of the impressive Bulleid coaches which is the fourth vehicle from the engine.

Plate 113 (right upper): A push-pull train en route for Bournemouth West at Holmsley, first station after leaving the main line at Lymington Junction, on 30th August 1961. The track bed is now part of a main road. The set, No. 662, is in rather poor condition with paint peeling from the driving unit.

Plate 114 (right lower): Standard Class 4MT No. 76029 on a freight train to Brockenhurst near Ashley Heath on the morning of 11th April 1964. There were 37 of these engines allocated to the Southern Region, the majority of which were based at Eastleigh.

THE RINGWOOD BRANCH

The line was double track throughout and ran in an arc north of the Waterloo–Weymouth main line between Brockenhurst and Poole. It was usually push-pull operated, most trains running from Brockenhurst to Bournemouth West. It served the market towns of Ringwood and Wimborne, the former being the junction for a line running south to Christchurch which was closed in 1935. West Moors was the junction for the line to Salisbury and Broadstone Junction marked the beginning of the Somerset and Dorset Railway line to Bath.

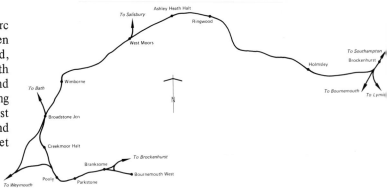

Plate 112: When push-pull sets were pushed, any non-fitted vehicles had to be coupled behind the engine. On the evening of 7th June 1960, a train is seen arriving at Brockenhurst from Bournemouth West with set No. 385.

Plate 115 (above): On the same day a Bournemouth based Class 4MT No. 76019 leaves Ashley Heath Halt on the 9.32 am from Brockenhurst. This train ran only as far as Wimborne. The halt was opened by the Southern Railway in 1927.

Plate 116: Extraordinary motive power for a local train. Rebuilt 'West Country' Class No. 34045 *Ottery St. Mary* on a two-coach Maunsell set at Ringwood. This formed the 4.34 pm Bournemouth West–Brockenhurst on 18th April 1964.

Plate 117: Standard Class 3MT No. 82026 on the 10.30 am Poole–Brockenhurst near Wimborne on 11th April 1964. Although the line lost its passenger service the following month, a freight service was retained from Bournemouth as far as Wimborne for several more years.

Plate 118: Early afternoon on 30th August 1961 saw considerable activity at Wimborne with Standard Class 4MT No. 76015 and push-pull set No. 613 leaving on the 2.08 pm from Brockenhurst. Class N No. 31814 is shunting a pick-up freight from Salisbury.

Plate 119 (above): On 30t
August 1961, Class M7 N
30050 joins the SDJR line from
Bath at Broadstone Junction with
the 5.05 pm Brockenhurst–
Bournemouth West.

Plate 120: The same train
Broadstone Junction Station. T
leading van is the ubiquitous S
utility van, of which many hun
dreds were built. Design varie
little over the years, the one c
this train being one of t
plywood-sided type built by BR

Plate 121: Standard Class 3MT No. 82029 on a Bournemouth-bound train between Broadstone Junction and Poole on the evening of 18th April 1964. The line on the left went to Hamworthy Junction, thus enabling trains to bypass Bournemouth. By this time the writing was on the wall, or rather the body side, for even the Maunsell coaches. The beginning of a long line of condemned coaches is seen on the left.

Plate 122 (below): Class M7 No. 30111 approaches Bournemouth West on the 12.08pm from Brockenhurst on 10th September 1959. In the background are the carriage sidings which provided stock for the Waterloo main line, local and SDJR services. Note the different design of signals on the gantry in the foreground. The distant arms are SR fluted pattern, whereas the home, again SR, is flat faced. The edge is lipped to give rigidity. The gantry itself is probably of LSWR origin.

THE ISLE OF WIGHT

The Isle of Wight has always found favour with railway enthusiasts, with its frequent services operated by ex-LSWR Class 02 tank engines and almost exclusively pre-grouping rolling stock. Even today, the remnants of the system are interesting in that passenger stock consists of ex-London Transport underground coaches.

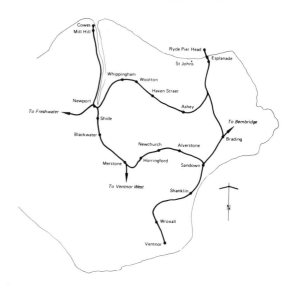

Plate 123: Class 02 No. W22 *Brading* on a Ryde—Cowes train passing the engine shed and carriage sidings at Newport on 12th August 1965. The 02s were introduced to the Island in 1923. They were modified by having enlarged coal bunkers and Westinghouse brake gear. There were eventually 23 of the class on the Island, together with four ex-LBSCR Class E1 0-6-0 tanks for freight trains. Newport was the starting point for Yarmouth trains which were worked by Class A1X. This line was closed in 1953.

Plate 124 (right upper): A van train in the bay at Newport with Class 02 No. W21, minus nameplate, on 20th ▶ September 1965. The SR utility vans were the most modern stock on the Island. Most of the wagons were ex-LBSCR and the coaches were LBSCR and SECR.

Plate 125 (right lower): Class 02 No. W24 *Calbourne* pauses at Ashley on the 5.30 pm Ryde—Cowes at the height of ▶ the holiday season on 22nd August 1960. The set number is 486, but unlike the mainland, set formations were frequently changed. In the foreground is the remains of the passing loop which was taken out in 1926.

Plate 126 (left upper): Freight trains were only infrequently seen in daylight hours. Class O2 No. W20 *Shanklin* passes Haven Street on a train from Medina Wharf to Ryde St. John's on 12th August 1965. Haven Street was made a passing place when the Ashey loop was removed. Medina Wharf was the main point of entry for coal and heavy goods, including railway stock, from the mainland.

Plate 127 (left lower): Departure from Mill Hill, last stop before Cowes, on 12th August 1965. The line from Newport to Cowes was the first section of the Isle of Wight Central Railway and was opened 13 years before services ran right through to Ryde in 1875.

The Sandown—Newport line was opened in 1879 and became part of the IWCR in 1887. One station was still issuing IWCR excess fare tickets in 1955! This reflects either the honesty of the passengers over the years or great foresight on the part of the IWCR in printing sufficient tickets to last the lifetime of the line.

Plate 128: Class 02 No. W31 *Chale* at Merstone on a wet December day in 1955, one week prior to closure of the line. Merstone was formerly the junction for the Ventnor West line, closed three years previously.

RYDE–VENTNOR

The main route to Ryde from the mainland was, and still is, from Portsmouth. There was, until 1913, a competing service from Stokes Bay, a spur from the Gosport line, connecting with LSWR trains from London (see *Plates 39-41*). From Ryde Pier Head to the town, passengers had the choice of catching the train, the pier tramway, walking or even driving. Walking was the most entertaining, as one could photograph all the other modes of propulsion in operation.

Plate 129 (below): Ryde Pier Head was therefore the scene of much activity, particularly on summer Saturdays on arrival of the ferry. The train for Ventnor departed first, followed a few minutes later by the Cowes train. The photograph was taken on 14th May 1961.

Plate 130 (right upper): A train from Cowes approaches Ryde St. John's, with a down train headed by No. W14 *Fishbourne* ► ready to leave on 12th August 1965. This was the original terminus of the Ventnor line, opened in 1864, and services were not extended to Ryde Esplanade and Pier Head until 1880.

Plate 131 (right lower): There was a substantial climb from Ryde St. John's. Class O2 No. W28 *Ashey* on the 6.05 pm to ► Ventnor approaches Smallbrook Junction on 4th August 1959, where the Cowes and Ventnor lines diverge. In the summer months the two lines from Ryde St. John's to the junction were operated as conventional up and down lines. In the winter, one line was used only for Ventnor trains and the other for Cowes trains.

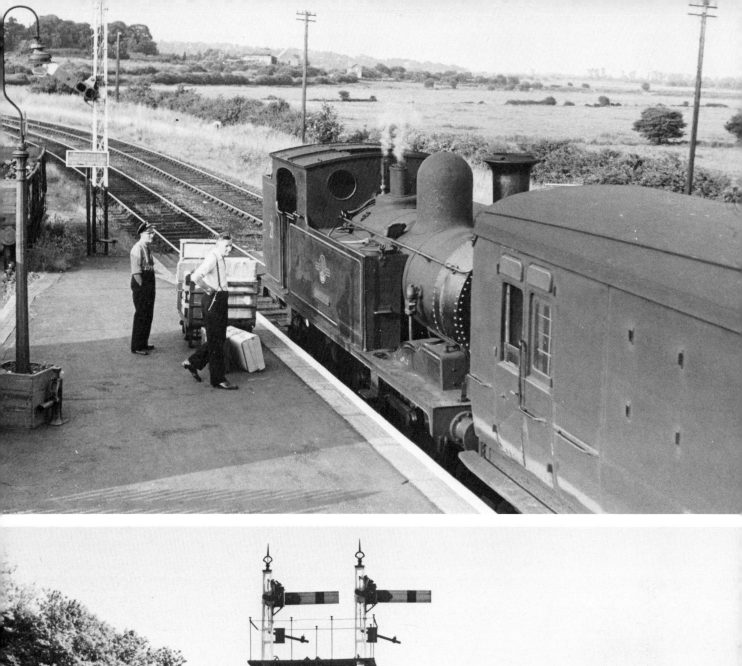

Plate 132 (left upper): Class O2 No. W21 *Sandown* on the 6.20 pm Ventnor–Ryde pauses at Brading on 5th July 1964. At one time this was the junction for the short branch to Bembridge. There was even a ferry from Bembridge to Langston on Hayling Island shortly after the line opened, but this did not survive for long.

Plate 133 (left lower): Ventnor was approached through a tunnel 1,312 yards long through the chalk face of St. Boniface Down. The tunnel began virtually at the platform end and rose at 1 in 173 towards Ryde. This was one good reason for running engines bunker first towards Ryde, a convention maintained throughout the Island.

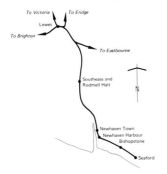

THE SEAFORD BRANCH

Seaford was unusual, in that its services began and ended on branch lines. Trains, consisting of 2-NOL and in later years 2-BIL electric units, ran from Seaford to Lewes, then along the main line to Haywards Heath and terminated at Horsted Keynes, the present northern terminus of the Bluebell Railway.

Plate 134 (above): Very rarely was the Seaford branch included in steam rail tours, but on 7th October 1962 Classes A1X No. 32636 and E6 No. 32418 are seen leaving Lewes. The E6 class was designed by Billinton for freight work and it was unusual to see them on passenger trains.

Plate 135: Class E4 No. 32479 shunting the stock of the special at Seaford. The E4 0-6-2 tank was also designed by Billinton as a mixed traffic engine. There were originally 75 in the class and even in the late 1950s they were a common sight on the Brighton section. By the end of 1962 there were only five left, all except one being allocated to Brighton shed. The remaining one was sold to the Bluebell Railway, where it can still be seen today.

Plate 136: The return train near Seaford behind Nos. 32418 and 32636 again. Originally Class A1, No. 32636 was built in 1872 as No. 72 *Fenchurch*. It was sold by the LBSCR in 1898, but later rebuilt as Class A1X and returned to the SR, to become No. 636.

THE SEATON BRANCH

In contrast to Lyme Regis (*Plates 93-98*), the Seaton branch was flat, straight and had mediocre scenery, but was nevertheless worth a visit. It was opened in 1868 and had two intermediate stations, Colyton and Colyford. Part of the track bed, between Colyford and Seaton, is now used by an electrically operated tramway to a gauge of 2 ft. 9 in. The tramcars are two-thirds the size of their prototypes.

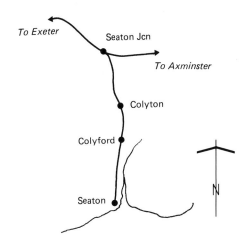

Plate 137 (below): In between branch trips the engine of the day, in this case Class M7 No. 30048, was used for shunting in the milk depot at Seaton Junction. After closure of the branch on 7th March 1966, Seaton Junction itself was also closed to passengers, but continued to handle milk traffic for some years.

Plate 138 (overleaf): Back on the branch train on the same day, 8th August 1960, is No. 30048 with set No. 603 at Seaton Junction. The all-third, No. 1050, used to strengthen the set is now preserved.

Plate 141 (below:) The terminus at Seaton, with a single road engine shed on the left, and the branch train on 8th August 1960. The original station buildings were replaced by the Southern Railway. The line saw little freight and relied heavily on holiday traffic. There were through trains to Waterloo for many years and through coaches can be seen on the right. Through services ceased in 1963.

Plate 139 (left upper:) Class M7 No. 30048 again, with the branch set and a corridor coach on the rear. This will form the through coach from Seaton—Waterloo the following morning, 9th August 1960.

Plate 140 (left lower:) No. 30048 passing the outer home at Seaton Junction on 8th August 1960. Locomotives as large as 'West Countries' were permitted to work on the line. Regular steam operation ceased at the end of 1963 and was replaced by diesel multiple units until closure.

SHEERNESS-ON-SEA BRANCH

The Isle of Sheppey once had four lines, radiating from Queenborough and beyond. This was the first station on the Island on the line from Sittingbourne. The main attraction, from the railway's point of view, was the presence of the docks at Sheerness. Apart from Sheerness itself, the only line of any length was that to Leysdown which was known as the Sheppey Light Railway. The Leysdown branch was worked by SECR steam rail motors, whose bodies were later converted to a two-coach articulated set. The line closed in 1950, but the set was used for some years afterwards on other parts of the Southern Region. Two of the other branches (Sheerness Dockyard and Queenborough Pier) closed at grouping, but the Sheerness line itself was electrified in 1959 and is still in operation.

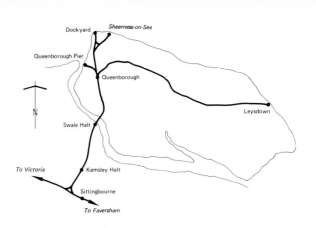

Plate 142 (above): Class 2MT No. 41313 is seen leaving Sittingbourne, on the Kent coast main line, on the 10.19 am to Sheerness on 12th March 1959. The stock is a Maunsell TO and BR standard coaches. There were through workings from Victoria.

Plate 143 (left): The line was worked by a variety of motive power, mostly provided by Gillingham and Faversham sheds. Class C No. 31112 is seen at Sheerness with ex-SECR and LSWR stock on the 3.20 pm to Sittingbourne on 7th October 1956.

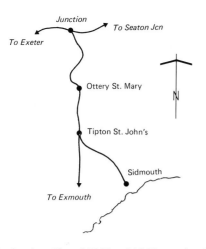

THE SIDMOUTH BRANCH

Sidmouth was served by a direct line from Sidmouth Junction on the West of England main line and also from Exmouth. Exmouth trains were obliged to reverse at Tipton St. John's. There were also occasional trains direct from Sidmouth Junction to Exmouth and in common with all branches in the area, through trains from Waterloo. The original station, on the site of the junction for Sidmouth, was called Feniton. It was known as Sidmouth Junction throughout the existence of the branch, but reverted to the name Feniton after closure. Feniton still has a train service direct from Waterloo.

Plate 144 (below): Class M7 No. 30323 on the 3.38 pm Exmouth–Sidmouth, prior to running round, at Tipton St. John's on 24th August 1958. Note the miscellaneous stock, comprising an LMSR TK, a Southern BTK and an all-third.

Plate 145 (left upper):   The same train climbing out of Tipton St. John's towards Sidmouth on 24th August 1958. The line climbs at 1 in 45 for two miles and then falls for the last mile into Sidmouth. Unfortunately the terminus is three-quarters of a mile from the sea front.

Plate 146 (left lower):   The Class M7 tanks were virtually displaced from Exmouth Junction duties by ex-LMSR and Standard tanks, and these in turn by diesel units in 1963. Class 2MT No. 41306 arrives at Sidmouth on the 10.36 am from Tipton St. John's on 9th August 1960.

Plate 147 (above):   Another Class 2MT leaving Sidmouth the same day, with the 10.20 am. This train consists of the branch stock and two through coaches for Waterloo. The Waterloo service continued until the end of the summer season in 1965. The branch itself was closed f111 1967. Note the LSWR wooden-post signal, now fitted with upper quadrant SR arms.

THE SWANAGE BRANCH

A well-patronised branch ran to Swanage, relying both on holiday traffic and freight in the form of Purbeck stone and china clay. There was a regular passenger service connecting with main line trains at Wareham and in the summer months there were through trains both from Waterloo and occasionally from other regions. The line survived the 'Beeching' era, but finally closed in 1972. Part of the line is the subject of a preservation scheme, which like Westerham some years previously is threatened with plans to use part of the track bed for a new road.

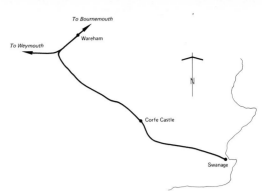

Plate 149 (above): The same formation passing Worgret Junction signal box, where the branch line leaves the former LSWR main line to Weymouth.

Plate 150 (right): Push-pull stock was normally used, even if the engine was not so fitted. Class 3MT No. 82029 hauling set No. 604 near Wareham on 11th April 1964.

Plate 148 (left): On 11th April 1964, Standard Class 3MT No. 82029 is seen on the main line approaching Worgret Junction on the 12.04 pm Wareham—Swanage. The junction signal is of SR design using bullhead rail for the main post and lattice work of LSWR pattern for the remainder.

Plate 151 (left upper): Class M7 No. 30053 on another Maunsell push-pull set passing Furzebrook Sidings on the 1.40 pm from Swanage on 11th April 1964.

Plate 153 (right): Some trains originated from Bournemouth Central. Seen here is Class 3MT No. 82026 near Worgret Junction on an evening train to Swanage. There was a much shorter route by road between Bournemouth and Swanage, but queues for the ferry across Poole Harbour meant that it was often quicker to use the train.

Plate 154 (below): Class M7 No. 30053 leaving Swanage on the 4.05 pm to Wareham on 11th April 1964. Although tank engines usually worked the branch train, it was quite common to see 'West Country' Pacifics or other express engines here.

THREE BRIDGES—EAST GRINSTEAD

An intensive push-pull service was run between Three Bridges and East Grinstead. When the line was built, East Grinstead was by far the more important of the two towns. The main purpose of Three Bridges was merely to serve as a junction for the London—Brighton line and for Horsham, also of considerable importance. Both London and Brighton could, however, also be reached from East Grinstead by direct services.

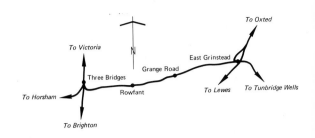

Plate 155 (below): At Three Bridges the branch train was afforded an all-over roof. Class H No. 31544 and a Maunsell set form the 10.27 am to East Grinstead on 7th October 1962.

Plate 156 (right upper): Class M7 No. 30055 with set No. 661 en route for East Grinstead at Rowfant on the evening of 3rd June 1960. Rowfant was one of the most picturesque and architecturally unusual stations in Sussex. There was also a fuel storage depot here, to the right of the photograph, but fortunately this was mostly underground.

Plate 157 (right lower): Class H No. 31306 on the 1.20 pm Three Bridges—East Grinstead entering Rowfant on 9th September 1961. The signalman is ready to exchange tablets.

Plate 160 (below): Another Farnborough special passes Grange Road, hauled by Class C2X No. 32523. Grange Road was originally called Grange Road for Crawley Down and Turner's Hill. By the time substantial housing development had begun at Grange Road itself, the closure of the line had been announced.

Plate 158 (left upper): Rowfant later the same day with Class H No. 31551 and set No. 606. Apart from the BR station nameplates, the station appears to be still in the 19th century, complete with ladders ready to light the oil lamps when evening approaches.

Plate 159 (left lower): Very rarely was anything larger than Turner 0-4-4 tank engine seen on the branch. Class K No. 32348 passes Class H No. 31551, the tender engine having worked a special train in connection with the Farnborough Air Show on 9th September 1961.

Plate 161: Class M7 No. 30109 approaches East Grinstead with ex-LBSCR stock, set No. 758, on the 10.49 am from Three Bridges on 2nd May 1958.

Plate 162: East Grinstead to Three Bridges trains were normally push-pull operated, but on the evening of 3rd March 1960 the push-pull stock was hauled by Class 4MT No. 80011, seen leaving East Grinstead.

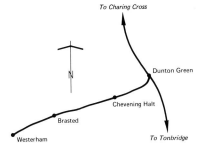

THE WESTERHAM BRANCH

The terminus at Westerham was only five miles from the London–Tonbridge main line at Dunton Green. It was opened in 1881 and had one intermediate station at Brasted. In BR days it had an hourly service, even on Sundays, and was invariably worked by an SECR Class H tank engine, chimney first, from Dunton Green.

Plate 163 (below): Class H No. 31519 with ex-LSWR stock at Westerham. The branch had seen considerable variety of motive power prior to grouping when it was worked by Class P 0-6-0 tanks and even by the larger tender engines of the SECR. After nationalisation ex-LCDR Classes R and R1 were used until their withdrawal (see *Plate 102*), whereupon the H tanks took over.

Plate 164 (left upper): For many years after conversion to push-pull operation, one of the ex-SECR rail motor sets worked the branch. Set No. 482 is seen stranded at Westerham, as the line was closed due to flooding on 2nd September 1958.

Plate 165 (left lower): Three weeks later, on 24th September 1958, with services resumed, Class H No. 31517 approaches Westerham. The train is composed of the same set with the addition of a horse box. In the foreground is the site of the engine shed, which was closed in 1906.

Plate 166 (right): The inevitable closure notice. Despite vigorous attempts to re-open the line as a commuter service and weekend steam railway, the stations were demolished and the track lifted in 1967 pending the building of a new road near Brasted.

Plate 167 (below): The weekend of closure saw a suitably decorated Class H No. 31518 on the regular passenger service.

CLOSURE OF WESTERHAM BRANCH RAILWAY LINE

. . . .

On and from MONDAY, 30th OCTOBER, 1961 all passenger and freight train services will be withdrawn from the branch line between DUNTON GREEN and WESTERHAM. CHEVENING HALT, BRASTED HALT and WESTERHAM station WILL BE CLOSED.

British Railways will continue to provide collection and delivery services for parcels and freight sundries traffic throughout the area and facilities for truck load traffic exist at other stations in the vicinity.

Further information may be obtained from the Station Masters at SEVENOAKS (Telephone 52231), or DUNTON GREEN (Telephone 325), or from the Line Traffic Manager, Southern Region, British Railways, South Eastern Division, 61 Queen Street, London, E.C.4 (Telephone WATerloo 5151, Ext. 227).

Alternative bus and coach facilities in the area are provided by the London Transport Executive and enquiries regarding these services should be addressed to London Transport Executive, 55 Broadway, London, S.W.1 (Telephone ABBey 1234) or any local office.

. . . .

⟨ SOUTHERN ⟩

Plate 168: Later the same day the push-pull workings were superseded by main line stock and more substantial motive power. Class D1 No. 31739 leaves Chevening Halt on the 2.50 pm Dunton Green-Westerham train.

INDEX OF LOCATIONS